Stop Paying Out!

How to save thousands during your divorce or when ending your civil partnership

Debbie Thomas

This book does exactly what it says in the title. Using plain English language and offering practical and evidence-based advice, this book really does help you to save money and only spend what you need to during painful and life-changing circumstances."

Francine Roberts

I love it. It's a positive message to anyone who needs to split up with their partner but is daunted by the costs and distress of the whole thing. It shows that if you make up your mind to stay calm and rational, and gain control by taking a methodical, step-by-step approach, you can resolve your break-up as well as possible, without risking all you have."

Hannah Renier

I think the book is excellent and I would have found something like this extremely helpful when I was going through my own divorce."

Sam Barker

ISBN: 978-1-9160445-0-0

A catalogue record of this book is available from the British Library.

CONTENTS

ABOUT THE AUTHOR

Debbie Thomas is a Professional McKenzie Friend (see Chapter 5 for more details about the work of a Professional McKenzie Friend) who works closely with families by providing assistance throughout their court proceedings when they do not have a lawyer.

Her journey towards professional McKenzie Friend work began in earnest some years ago after she dealt with her own complex family case and experienced first-hand the many challenges of the legal system in England – during a series of hearings lasting over 5 years.

Faced with unaffordable legal fees, she was forced to find ways to save money. She represented herself in court as a 'litigant in person'. Having achieved a successful outcome in her case, she went on to support others as an informal McKenzie Friend.

Debbie was awarded a postgraduate law degree in 2017. Before that, she worked as a freelance journalist for 10 years, covering UK and international case law and legal practice for legal journals and online publications including International Bar News, the Legal 500, the European Legal 500 and LexisNexis Butterworths Law Leader. She has also written extensively for financial and business publications.

Debbie is a full member of the Society of Professional McKenzie Friends and is committed to their code of conduct. She adheres to the Civil and Family Courts McKenzie Friend Practice Guidance.

To find out more about her work, visit:
www.goingtocourtalone.co.uk

PREFACE

There was a time when going through a divorce or civil partnership dissolution meant using lawyers for every part of the process – from start to finish. The inevitable outcome for both parties was a significant legal bill. And although times are changing, it can still be very easy for legal costs to spiral out of control.

In my work as a Professional McKenzie Friend, I'm regularly approached by clients who have spent eye-watering sums on ending their relationships and on related family matters, without getting anywhere near the end of the process. And in my own divorce, I had no option but to find ways to cut my legal costs to avoid financial ruin.

This book is designed to give you financial empowerment. And by that, I mean the power to control your divorce or your civil partnership dissolution finances by starting from a position of strength: knowledge.

I will show you practical ways to manage your costs, using the strategies I've used myself. And I'll show you how these strategies will help you to radically cut your spending, so that you do not pay any more than you want to, have to or are able to. I'll also show you how to get help for free.

While this book is not intended to detail every single aspect of ending a marriage, ending a civil partnership – nor of all the related financials (because every case is different and this area of law is complex and changes frequently), it contains a wealth of practical information I have gained through first-hand experience.

Although this publication focuses on the financials and related legal matters, your emotional health and personal safety are extremely important. If you are being abused in any way and/or suspect that your partner has a personality disorder, it is vital that you seek help immediately. Ensure that you have a good emotional support structure around you before, during and after the end of your relationship, but even then you may need outside help. You will find the contact details of organisations that serve this purpose in the resources section. Although the emotional journey falls outside of the remit of this work, there is no suggestion that its paramount importance is diminished.

You will also find other valuable sources of help in the resources section. Please use these resources in the context of your situation and based on whether they are the right fit for you and your circumstances.

This book is written with a UK audience in mind and legal references are based on the legal system of England and Wales. If you're located outside of these countries, you can still apply the tips and information to your situation, in accordance with the laws where you live.

This book will discuss money-saving in a practical, jargon-free way. It is by no means intended as a substitute for professional legal or financial advice, but it will give you a practical steer and will help you to save thousands.

Debbie Thomas

hello@goingtocourtalone.co.uk

CHAPTER 1
An amicable split can save you money

There are many reasons why an amicable split is beneficial, but one of the main reasons is money.

If you can continue to speak to each other and communicate effectively during your divorce or civil partnership dissolution – and reach an agreement and stick to that agreement – you will both reap the financial benefits.

There are a number of areas that you can both discuss and come to an agreement about.

Ending your marriage: divorce

If you've been married for at least 1 year, one of you can apply for a divorce. The application is in 3 parts.

The first part is to apply for the divorce. When applying, you must show that the marriage has broken down to a point where the relationship cannot be repaired (known as divorce on the ground that the marriage has broken down irretrievably).

You do this by choosing one or more reasons (known as facts) why the marriage cannot be saved. At the time of writing, there are 5 reasons: adultery, behaviour (formerly known as 'unreasonable behaviour'), desertion, separation for more than 2 years (if you both agree to the divorce) and separation for at least 5 years (whether or not you both agree to the divorce).

In general terms, the reason you choose will have no impact on your financial agreements.

You'll need to provide supporting information for whichever reason you choose.

The second part is to apply for the decree nisi. You can do this if your husband or wife agrees to the divorce. If the court is satisfied that the irretrievable breakdown of the marriage has been proved, it will issue a decree nisi.

The third part of the process is to make the application for the decree absolute. This is done (by the person who applied for the divorce) 6 weeks and 1 day after the decree nisi has been granted. The decree absolute is the legal document that confirms you're no longer legally married.

You do not usually have to attend court at any stage of the application, unless one of you disagrees.

If you've been married for less than 1 year, you can apply for a legal separation (known as a judicial separation).

Worth knowing: If at the time of applying for the divorce, you think you might not agree on your finances, you should tick the box in the divorce application form to indicate that you want to apply for a financial order; a court order that stipulates how your money and assets will be divided (formerly known as ancillary relief). The court will take no further action until you make a separate, full application for a financial order. There are a number of financial orders a court can make, depending on your circumstances.

Arrangements for your children will also have to be sorted out separately.

Ending your civil partnership: dissolution

If you've been in a civil partnership for at least 1 year, one of you can apply to end the civil partnership (known as a civil partnership dissolution or dissolution). There are 3 parts to the process.

The first part is to fill in a dissolution application. When applying, you must show that the civil partnership has broken down to a point where the relationship cannot be repaired (known as dissolution on the ground that the civil partnership has broken down irretrievably).

You do this by choosing one or more reasons (known as facts) for making the application. At the time of writing, there are 4 reasons: behaviour (formerly known as 'unreasonable behaviour'), desertion, separation for more than 2 years (if you both agree to the dissolution) and separation for more than 5 years (whether or not you both agree to end the civil partnership).

You'll need to provide supporting information for whichever reason you choose.

The second part is to apply for a conditional order. You can do this if your partner agrees to end the civil partnership. If the court is satisfied that the irretrievable breakdown of the civil partnership has been proved, it will issue a conditional order.

The third part of the process is to apply for a final order (in other words, to make the conditional order final). If you are the one who applied for the conditional order, you must wait until 6 weeks after the date of the conditional order to apply for the final order. The final order is the legal document that confirms your civil partnership has legally ended.

You do not usually have to attend court for any stage of the application, unless one of you disagrees.

If you've been in a civil partnership for less than a year, you can apply for a separation order.

Worth knowing: If at the time of applying to end your civil partnership, you think you might not agree on your finances, you should tick the box in the dissolution application form to indicate that you want to apply for a financial order.

The court will take no further action until you make a separate application for a financial order. There are a number of financial orders a court can make, depending on your circumstances.

Arrangements for your children will also have to be sorted out separately.

Reach an agreement when ending your marriage or civil partnership

Save money by agreeing on these points:

- When to apply for the divorce/dissolution

- Who will apply for it?

- The reasons for ending the marriage or civil partnership

- What proof or supporting information to use for your reasons for ending the marriage or civil partnership

- How quickly you want to finalise the divorce/dissolution (taking into account the legal minimum timeframes)

- How you will communicate with each other throughout

- Having an early discussion about your children and your finances.

Worth knowing: Once your partner has applied to end the marriage or civil partnership, if you don't agree with the reasons and supporting information your partner has given, you can still reach an agreement about the areas mentioned above, by working together to make changes.

——

Applying for a maintenance order

You can apply for a maintenance order (for spousal maintenance – the money one partner pays to the other for maintenance) at any time, once divorce or dissolution proceedings are underway.

A maintenance order can be for a fixed period – of a few months or many years. It can be until a set point in the future, such as when the youngest child finishes their university education, or until either party remarries or starts a civil partnership. It can be open-ended, or it can be a joint lives order that lasts until either party dies.

Your children

Try to reach an agreement as a couple and focus on the best interests of your children, rather than focusing on what you want.

If you have older children, they will probably want to have a say about which parent they will be living with, and how often they will see the parent they do not live with.

Save money by agreeing on these points:

- Who your children will live with
- What sort of contact your children will have with the non-resident parent – for example: how, how often, when?

- Whether they will live with both of you – and if so, what will the split be, for example 50/50, weekdays/weekends, etc.?

- How contact and/or residence will be split during the school holidays, for birthdays and for religious and non-religious holidays

- How will you make changes to living or contact arrangements?

- The schools your children will attend

- Notice of holidays abroad, and passports.

The above is by no means an exhaustive list. It may work for you to have a very detailed approach to your agreements or to have a more flexible arrangement.

Worth knowing: A parenting plan (an agreement between you and your child's other parent about arrangements for your child, including who your child will live with, and contact arrangements with the non-resident parent), is a useful tool to help you work together on arrangements for your child.

Work on a parenting plan together. You will find a number of templates online including one produced by CAFCASS (Children and Family Court Advisory and Support Service), the body that safeguards and promotes the welfare of children involved in the family justice system in England (known as CAFCASS CYMRU in Wales).

CAFCASS parenting plan: https://www.cafcass.gov.uk/grown-ups/parents-and-carers/divorce-and-separation/parenting-plan/

—

Child maintenance

Child maintenance payments are made by the parent who does not have day-to-day care of their child. These payments are a contribution towards a child's everyday living costs. If you both share day-to-day care, you can reach an agreement about your shared contributions towards your child's upkeep.

You can estimate your child maintenance contributions using this calculator: https://www.gov.uk/calculate-your-child-maintenance

If you can reach an agreement together, use Child Maintenance Options to help you put your agreement in writing: https://www.cmoptions.org/en/maintenance/

The family home

For many couples, the family home that once housed one family unit must now stretch to cover (or at least contribute towards) the cost of two separate homes.

Sometimes there isn't enough available to cover two homes. Often, the parent the children will be living with (or will be living with for the majority of the time), will be the one to remain in the family home. It may be that the family home has to be sold.

Explore the options together.

Save money by discussing – and agreeing on these points:

- Do you know how much the family home is worth?

- Do you need to get an up-to-date valuation on your home? Get 3 valuations done and agree together which one you will use.

- Will you sell the family home now or at an agreed date in the future?

- Will one of you buy the other out?

- If you sell the family home, how will you split the net proceeds of sale (the money that's left from the sale of the property – after all the costs of sale have been deducted)?

- Which one of you will manage the sale of the property?

- If you're not selling the family home now, who will live in it?

- Will the partner who will live in the family home with the children do so until the children finish school (or university)?

Worth knowing: If you can reach an agreement about your home, you can make it into a legally-binding financial settlement between you and your ex-partner by applying for a consent order. You can make the application for a consent order to the court yourselves (or contact a solicitor to make the application for you).

Any other assets or finances (see below) should be included in the consent order. You can include spousal maintenance in your consent order.

Be aware of the special timeframe that applies to your consent order (and to other financial orders). You can only get your consent order approved by a court if you've already started the paperwork to end your marriage or civil partnership and you have not applied for your decree absolute (to end your marriage) or final order (to end your civil partnership).

Make sure you have full details of all of your ex-partner's finances (known as full and frank financial disclosure) before agreeing to a consent order.

Get full and frank financial disclosure

Full and frank financial disclosure is a two-way process that involves you and your ex-partner providing a clear picture of your finances by sharing all of your financial information with each other.

Details to share with each other (for example when completing your form E – the form used for a financial order) include:

- Recent valuations of properties you own, and recent statements of any mortgages

- Recent valuations for all your pensions

- Valuations of savings accounts and investments (for example, shares)

- All accounts for any businesses you own

- All payslips

- The last 12 months' worth of all bank statements (personal and business).

Worth knowing: Financial proceedings rely on the full and frank disclosure of financial information and it is a criminal offence to get rid of any assets you have as a way of preventing someone from claiming what they are entitled to (known as dissipating assets so as to defeat the other party's claim).

Where assets have been transferred, for example from a joint account to a different account, a court can make an order to undo the transfer, and return the assets to where they were originally. It is also possible to apply for a freezing order to prevent assets being disposed of.

If your financial affairs are highly complex and involve significant sums of money, you may wish to consider using the specialist services of a forensic accountant to review your ex-partner's financial disclosure.

When preparing your case, be aware that if you take and use confidential documents belonging to your ex-partner without his or her consent, you could face prosecution for theft, burglary or breaching your ex-spouse's confidentiality.

Avoid paying extra property tax

Beware of the financial impact of becoming an 'accidental landlord'. Here's how this could happen.

You move out of the family home (property A), you let out property A, buy another property (property B) and live in property B. Unless you sell property A within 18 months of moving out of it, you will have to pay Capital Gains Tax (CGT) – a tax payable on a second property that is not your main residence. The amount of CGT you will have to pay will be based on the increase in the value of the property after you stopped living in it. CGT is payable because you didn't live in property A all of the time you owned it – and it is, therefore, classed as a second home.

Changes to Private Residence Relief (PRR) are due to come into force in 2020 and when they do, you will have only 9 months to sell the family home (property A) under these circumstances, before having to pay CGT. CGT is charged at 18% (for basic-rate taxpayers) and at 28% (for higher-rate taxpayers).

Other family assets and finances

The legal starting point for dividing up your assets is a 50/50 split, but in practical terms, other factors will come into play. These factors come under the general heading of the 'needs of the parties', in other words, what you both need, based on your individual circumstances – and the needs of any children under 18.

Other factors such as age, length of the marriage or civil partnership and earning capacity may also be taken into account.

Start by drawing up a full list of everything you own such as other properties, businesses, cars and anything else. These should not only be assets in England and Wales but also assets in other countries.

Include financial products such as bank accounts, savings, insurance policies, endowments, investments and pensions.

Be sure to include details of any debts you may have, for example, overdrafts, credit cards, secured or unsecured loans etc.

Prepare to sort out your pensions

Steps to take, based on your individual circumstances.

Find all the pensions you and your partner have and use the Pension Tracing Service to find lost pensions: https://www.gov.uk/find-pension-contact-details

Get a cash equivalent transfer value (CETV) from your pension scheme administrators – to find out the lump-sum equivalent value of your pension (do this as soon as possible to avoid delays).

Check the pension information provided by your employer and/or pension provider, including your yearly pension statement.

Check how much is in your pension (also known as getting a pension valuation):
https://www.pensionwise.gov.uk/en/pension-pot-value

Check the options for dividing up your pension:
https://www.moneyadviceservice.org.uk/en/articles/dividing-pensions-on-divorce-or-dissolution

Apply for a valuation of a state pension (after receiving the cash equivalent valuation):
https://www.gov.uk/government/publications/application-for-a-state-pension-forecast-on-divorce-or-dissolution-br20

Speak to a financial adviser (who is registered with the FCA – Financial Conduct Authority) about your pension options.
https://register.fca.org.uk/

Draw up an individual financial plan and include your income and outgoings (as well as payments towards debts). Take into account your needs plus the current and future needs of your children, and include any maintenance payments that you are or will be receiving from your ex-partner (or any maintenance payments you are or will be making). Include any state benefits you receive or are entitled to.

You'll find more details about how to track your expenditure in Chapter 3.

Your financial plan will help you to get a full picture of your needs and will give you a context on which to base how you (agree to) divide your assets and finances.

Next, look at your family assets and finances together and decide how to split these between you, based on the details in your individual financial plans.

If your financial affairs are complex, you may need to get help from an accountant or another financial professional.

Once you've reached a financial agreement that is fair and acceptable to you both, you can make it into a legally-binding financial settlement between you and your partner by applying for a consent order.

You can make the application to the court for a consent order yourselves (or contact a solicitor to make the application for you). Any other assets such as the family home (see family home above) should be included in the consent order.

Make sure you have full details of all of your ex-partner's finances (known as full and frank financial disclosure) before agreeing to a consent order. (see above for more details about getting full and frank financial disclosure).

Save money by agreeing on these points:

- How to divide all property and other assets in a way that is fair to you, your partner and your children
- Your financial needs based on your life after your divorce/dissolution
- How to divide any properties you own, based on your needs
- How to divide any savings, interest or investments between you, based on your needs
- Spousal maintenance payments
- How long spousal maintenance payments will be made for
- Child maintenance payments
- Pension-sharing arrangements.

Worth knowing: If there are to be no ongoing financial ties between you both (for example, no maintenance payments or no pension sharing), you may wish to consider a clean break order. A clean break order legally ends all financial ties between you both – for good.

—

Consider severing all financial ties

Without a clean break order, it means that in the future, one of you could apply to a court for a share of any financial gains the other has made, for example, income from a successful business, an inheritance, a lottery win or other windfall.

CHAPTER 2
Save on what you have to pay for

To assist with your planning, this chapter will discuss what you have to pay for – over and above the items in your financial plan (as discussed in Chapter 1). It also deals with some alternatives you may wish to consider.

Before paying for anything, first check whether you can get financial help.

Legal aid

Legal aid is help from the government to meet the cost of legal advice, family mediation and representation in court.

Eligibility for legal aid depends on your circumstances (for example, if your earnings are below a certain threshold or you receive some types of benefits).

Check whether you can apply for legal aid:
https://www.gov.uk/check-legal-aid

Worth knowing: If you do qualify for legal aid, be sure to contact legal advisers or mediators who handle legal aid cases. During my discussions with solicitors, I found that law firms, at the time, were less and less inclined to take on legal aid cases.

Some firms that do take on legal aid work will only do so if such cases are handled by specific solicitors.

This could further reduce your ability to access legal aid, even if you were to qualify for it.

Search for a legal adviser or a mediator who deals with legal aid: https://find-legal-advice.justice.gov.uk

Mediation and your MIAM appointment

Mediation is a lower-cost way to resolve difficulties (compared to taking issues straight to solicitors and the courts), and it may be a good money-saving option for you, depending on your situation. A family mediator is an independent and professionally trained mediator who can work with you and your ex-partner to help you reach an agreement about issues that you are facing.

If you intend to take your case to court, you must, in most cases, ensure that you attend an initial mediation appointment. Known as the Mediation Information Assessment Meeting (MIAM), this appointment is run by a certified mediator (who holds a Family Mediation Council Accreditation). The mediator will assess whether mediation can be used to resolve your difficulties.

There is a fee to pay for your MIAM, unless you qualify for legal aid.

If your MIAM goes well and you all (you, your ex-partner and the mediator) agree that mediation is right for you, you should book in your mediation sessions.

There will be fees to pay for each mediation session you attend (unless you qualify for legal aid) and you can save money by comparing the fees of mediators and weighing up the quoted fees against the duration and location of each session.

After your MIAM, your mediator will give you a signed form, or sign your (court application) form to prove to the court that you attended a MIAM.

Check and compare the price of MIAMs online. Some factors that will affect the amount you pay for your MIAM include location, whether you attend separately or together, and whether the session is run in person or online.

Find a mediator: https://www.familymediationcouncil.org.uk/

MIAM exemptions

In some cases, you do not have to attend a MIAM and you can get a MIAM exemption. Exemptions apply where, for example, there has been domestic violence between you both – and the police and courts have been involved.

See a full list of MIAM exemptions under Part 3 of the Family Procedure Rules: http://www.justice.gov.uk/courts/procedure-rules/family/parts/part_03#para3.8

Family arbitration

To save time and money, you can both appoint an arbitrator to work with you to resolve any family disputes or issues.

An arbitrator is a family justice professional who will listen to what you both have to say, and look at the facts and evidence, before making a decision that is final and binding.

Arbitration is a form of dispute resolution (resolving differences between two parties) and can be a cost-effective alternative to going to court because the dispute can be settled in a shorter time.

Arbitrators generally charge a fixed-fee for their services.

Find an arbitrator: http://ifla.org.uk

Collaborative law

If you are able to communicate, work together and trust each other, a financially-attractive alternative to court procedures is collaborative law.

Collaborative law involves working as a couple with your own collaborative lawyer to find solutions to problems, using open lines of communication and finding creative solutions.

It can save you money by avoiding the expense of preparing for court hearings. Fixed-fee arrangements may be made in some cases.

Find a collaborative lawyer: http://www.resolution.org.uk/findamember/

Court fees

In most cases, there is a fee to pay for an application to the court (for a court order). You must pay the fee when you send your application to the court otherwise, the court will not process your application.

Applications and court orders include:

- Application for a divorce, dissolution or (judicial) separation
- Child arrangements order
- Consent order
- Financial order

Worth knowing: Some family orders carry no court fee, for example an occupation order or a non-molestation order.

Some court forms, for example, the application for a divorce, dissolution or (judicial) separation, are available as an electronic form that can be filled in and submitted online. Most court forms are available online (but are not electronic). Such forms can be filled in and downloaded or printed off, and can be sent by email to the court or by post, or can be delivered by hand.

Find all the court forms online: https://www.gov.uk/government/collections/court-and-tribunal-forms

Help with court fees

If you have few or no savings, receive state benefits or are on a low income, you might be able to get money off your court fees.

Use form EX160 to apply for help with court fees: https://www.gov.uk/government/publications/apply-for-help-with-court-and-tribunal-fees#details

You may also be able to get a refund on any court fees you have already paid in the three-month period prior to the date you send in your completed EX160 form.

Court fees increase periodically. You'll find a full list of current fees in form EX50: https://www.gov.uk/government/publications/fees-in-the-civil-and-family-courts-main-fees-ex50

Worth knowing: Check your completed forms carefully and sign them before sending them to the court. Make sure you read all of the guidance information for each form, follow the instructions and include any documents or copies of documents you have been asked to provide.

It may help to get a trusted friend with an eye for detail to check your form over for you. The court will not give you a refund if you have made a mistake on your form – and you might have to make a new application and pay the fee again.

Legal representation

Before you look for legal representation, check whether you qualify for legal aid. If you do qualify for legal aid, it may cover all or part of your legal fees. If you do not qualify for legal aid, shop around and compare fees.

Solicitors

Solicitors are responsible for managing a case, giving advice, preparing documents for court and appointing and briefing a barrister. When you instruct (appoint) a solicitor to work on your case, you must pay a fee.

Solicitors mostly work in law firms and each law firm has its own fee structure, based on the location and size of the law firm – and the seniority of the solicitor.

Solicitors will confirm their fees in a client care letter after your first meeting. That first meeting is generally charged at a set rate. Some firms offer a free initial consultation.

Find a solicitor: http://solicitors.lawsociety.org.uk

Barristers

Barristers are also known as advocates and work in Chambers (barristers offices) as independent specialist lawyers. Some are self-employed. They focus on giving advice and advocacy (putting a case across in court or in writing).

You must pay fees when you instruct a barrister to work on your case. The fee a barrister charges is based on years of experience after they have qualified as a barrister.

It is now possible for members of the public to go direct when instructing a barrister (known as direct access or public access barristers), without having to go through a solicitor.

By instructing a barrister directly, you can save money by not paying for the services of a solicitor.

The Direct Access Portal will give you a list of barristers who will accept your instruction.

Find a public access barrister: www.barcouncil.org.uk/publicaccess

Chartered Legal Executives

Chartered Legal Executives or Chartered Legal Executive Lawyers mostly work in law firms and are similar to solicitors.

The difference between a Chartered Legal Executive and a solicitor is that a Chartered Legal Executive has qualified as a lawyer and has been trained to specialize as an expert in one or two areas of law (whereas solicitors have undergone a broader and more general legal training).

Chartered Legal Executives can, therefore, do the work of a solicitor and, in some situations, are responsible for supervising solicitors.

Using a Chartered Legal Executive may save you money. Check by comparing rates.

Find a Chartered Legal Executive: https://www.cilex.org.uk/about_cilex/about-cilex-lawyers/cilex-practitioners-directory

Worth knowing: When deciding on a lawyer, consider whether you would benefit from expertise in a particular area. For example, if your finances are complicated, consider a family solicitor who specializes in divorce or dissolution finances.

Weigh up the cost and benefits of paying more for a specialist, versus paying less for more generalist advice. It could have an impact on the amount of money you receive or have to pay out after your divorce or dissolution.

Value-added tax

VAT (value-added tax) is a tax that all VAT-registered businesses and individuals charge their customers and pay to HMRC (HM Revenue & Customs).

Law firms and barristers that are VAT-registered will do the same. VAT is currently charged at 20%.

You'll have to pay VAT on top of your legal fees when VAT is charged. Check your lawyer's fees to see whether VAT is included and factor this in when checking or comparing fees. VAT is generally listed separately alongside the fee as '+ VAT'.

CHAPTER 3

How to put more money into your pocket

During this period of your life, your financial situation is likely to change. The best way to prepare for the changes ahead is to assess your finances as soon as possible – and work on a plan for your future financial needs.

To assess your current finances, you'll need the full answer to at least 3 questions: What is your total income? How much are you spending? What do you spend your money on?

When looking at your income, include all sources, such as your salary, any benefits or payments from other sources (for example, maintenance from a partner, child benefit, or a pension). When it comes to outgoings, it's important to think, not just about the main or big-ticket items you pay for each month, such as the mortgage or rent, council tax, gas and electricity – but also the other items you need money for, however trivial the individual amounts may seem.

The same applies when planning for your financial future when you are no longer married or in a civil partnership. Based on your circumstances, your spending in some areas is likely to change. For example, you may have to pay all of your rent or mortgage yourself.

Slash your council tax bill

If you're the only adult living in your property, you're entitled to receive a 25% reduction in your council tax (until any child living with you reaches the age of 18, or another adult moves in).

You'll have to ask your local authority for the reduction (known as a 'single person council tax discount'); it won't be given to you automatically!

If you're on a low income or receive benefits, you may be entitled to a council tax reduction (formerly known as 'council tax benefit'). Depending on your circumstances, the reduction could be as much as 100%.

To apply for a council tax reduction, go to: https://www.gov.uk/apply-council-tax-reduction

Putting together a complete list of all your current financial commitments and future financial requirements may take some time, but it will be time well spent.

Worth knowing: You'll need to do all of the above and more if you're applying for a financial order.

When preparing for your financial order, double check your figures to make sure they are right, so that you do not lose out financially.

How to track your expenditure

Tracking your expenditure is an essential part of building up a complete picture of your financial needs. It's the best way to put money back into your pocket for a number of reasons.

By tracking your spending and financial commitments you're gathering valuable evidence, and this will stand you in good stead, whether you're negotiating the financials with your ex-partner, or preparing to provide financial evidence to a court.

Your expenditure and financial commitments will tell you what you need. Without that knowledge, you may not be in the best position to ask for what you need and if you do not ask for what you need (and show why you need it), you may not get it.

To help get you started, you'll find a sample monthly expenditure list at the end of this chapter.

Bank statements

Start by looking at your bank statements (for all your bank and other financial accounts) covering the last 12 months and make a note of all the items you regularly pay for, as well as all your other regular or one-off items of expenditure.

Draw up a separate list for cash withdrawals.

Receipts

Go through as many recent receipts as possible. If you have a month's worth of receipts (or even a week's worth, if that's all you have), go through them to check what you've paid for in cash and match that evidence of spending against your list of cash withdrawals from your bank account.

Use the same approach to cross-reference receipts for card payments against the relevant bank accounts.

If you do not have enough receipts or have none at all, start keeping your receipts from today so that you can track your cash spending for at least a week. Get into the habit of asking for and keeping your printed receipts.

Many shops will offer to send your receipts to you digitally (in exchange for your email address), so be sure to accept this service, or ask for it, if you prefer to manage your finances digitally.

There is also a vast number of digital apps available that you can download from the internet to your smartphone. You can use these apps to scan, track and manage your receipts. You will also find websites or desktop versions of the apps that you can use on your computer.

Worth knowing: Keep a back-up copy of everything – whether your preferred tracking method is digital or paper-based.

Remember to track and keep records of everything. It's far better to have too much data than not enough, especially if you're dealing with the courts, or plan to.

You'll need to convert all the relevant digital records of your finances into printed copies if you are preparing documents to take to court as part of your court bundle (the file of documents you prepare and share with all parties and take to court to use during hearings).

Tools for tracking your expenditure

Apart from the old favourites, such as well-known word processing and spreadsheet software, there is a vast number of free and paid-for tools plus downloadable apps available, including online personal monthly budget templates.

You'll find budget and expenditure tools freely available online.

Financial tracking tools for your devices

There are numerous financial tracking tools for your smartphone that will allow you to sync your data to other devices such as your laptop or tablet, as well as your mobile phone.

Here are some of the commonly available features that you can use to track your spending.

You can:

- Automatically subtract recurring expenses and savings from your income
- Categorise your expenditure by type
- Carry out historical tracking: for example, tracking spending over a fixed period of time
- Receive text message alerts (as words or graphics) to show your spending patterns
- Track spending by type, month, or location.

Some tools can also be used to set a budget, set savings goals or even provide free access to your credit score.

Your credit score and your financial future

Knowing your credit score is particularly useful if you plan to apply for a financial product, such as a loan or a mortgage, in the near future. It's also useful to know whether there is a negative financial marker on your credit file.

For example, lettings agents tend to run a credit reference check before they will process a tenancy agreement.

Unless you have someone, who will stand as guarantor for your rent and for any other monies a landlord may be entitled to claim from you, it is better to find out first-hand about a bad credit file.

Worth knowing: You can check your credit reference file for any joint financial commitments or financial associations. Financial associations or links are created when you apply for a joint financial product with another person, such as a mortgage or bank account.

You may wish to consider getting a financial disassociation. A financial disassociation removes any financial link or association between you and another person, such as an ex-partner.

Contact one of the credit reference agencies to find out how to remove a financial link.

Monthly expenditure list

When you start to keep a record of your spending, you'll be surprised at the number of items of expenditure you'll discover you have, whether the items relate to recurring, one-off or unplanned spending.

Here's a sample monthly expenditure list to get you started.

You can download the sample list online from:
http://www.goingtocourtalone.co.uk/resources/

Sample expenditure list

After-school club
Appliance insurance
Appliances (repair, replacement)
Birthdays (gifts)
Bank (overdraft, charges)
Books (printed, digital and audio)
Building and contents insurance
Bus fares
Car breakdown cover
Car insurance
Car loan
Car maintenance (petrol, oil, repair)
Car parking
Car seats (for children)
Car servicing & MOT
Child clothing
Child travel fares
Clothing
Commuting
Computer (maintenance, repair and running costs)
Council tax
Credit card payments
Crockery
Decorating
Debt payments
Dentist
Electricity
Entertainment
Extra-curricular activities (music lessons, school trips, drama, dance)
Family breaks
Garden maintenance
Gas

General house maintenance and repairs
Groceries
Gym
Hairdressing
Household maintenance
Internet
Laptop (maintenance, repair and running costs)
Life insurance
Linen (pillows, sheets, quilts, quilt covers)
Loan payments
Medical expenses (prescriptions, jabs)
Mobile phone
Mortgage payments
Newspapers/journals
Optician (glasses, contact lenses)
Personal care
Pocket money
Printer (maintenance, repair and running costs e.g. ink cartridges, paper)
Pushchairs
Rail fares
Road tax
Rent
Rent deposit
School holiday club
School lunches/packed lunches
School uniform
Telephone
Travel insurance
TV – cable
TV licence
Water
Window cleaner

CHAPTER 4

Manage your lawyer, cut your costs

If you're in dispute or have to go to court to resolve matters, the area that you're likely to spend the most money on is legal fees.

Whichever type of legal representation you choose, whether you go for a solicitor, Chartered Legal Executive or barrister, there will be fees to pay.

Solicitors, Chartered Legal Executives and barristers tend to charge by the hour. For smaller pieces of work, such as short telephone calls or emails, a lawyer's fees may be based on a percentage of an hour, or a set rate for a certain number of minutes. You may find, for example, that if the set fee is for a unit of 6 minutes, you will have to pay for the full 6-minute unit, even if you only used 2 minutes.

How to save money

There are many ways that you can save money on your lawyer fees.

Compare fees

Compare fees before you instruct a lawyer to work on your case.

Think about value for money – and weigh up three factors: how much it will cost, how efficient the lawyer is and the quality of advice the lawyer is giving you.

Here are other ways to cut your costs:

Set a fee cap

If you have a ceiling on the amount you can spend, discuss this with your lawyer as soon as possible. They may be able to offer you a service that fits within your set budget.

For example, when setting a cap on how much you will pay, you can ask your lawyer to work until their fees reach the limit you've set. They'll contact you each time the cap has been reached.

You can use this method for a single piece of work only or for all the work your lawyer does for you.

Choose the fixed-fee option

Some lawyers provide work on a fixed-fee or agreed-fee basis; in other words, you pay a set amount for a specific piece of work.

A fixed-fee option is particularly useful when attending court hearings with your lawyer because hearings rarely run to time and it is common to spend hours waiting around in court on the day of your hearing. A fixed-fee option means, no matter how long you may have to wait, you know how much you'll be charged.

Worth knowing: for hearings, lawyers may make an additional charge for travel time and travel costs, such as car mileage and parking or rail travel.

Stop making repeated short phone calls

Once you've instructed a lawyer, limit the number of repeated short telephone calls you make to him or her, unless it's genuinely urgent. The same goes for firing off lots of short emails and letters to your lawyer.

Repeated short contact will be charged in set units of time and will end up costing you more. It's far more cost effective to gather all of your questions together and agree on a set amount of time to go through all of your questions and get your answers – in one go.

Use your lawyer – as a lawyer

Use your lawyer's time (and your money) for work relating to the legal side of your case only and try not to blur the lines by using your lawyer as a therapist.

Draw instead on your support network – such as a therapist, support group, best friend or family member for any emotional support you may need.

Keep a note of the work being done

It can be tempting to hand all your documents over to your lawyer and let them get on with it. The danger with this approach is you'll quickly lose sight of what's going on, and of the work being done.

Be as involved as possible by keeping a note of every piece of work you ask your lawyer to do for you, when you asked them to do it, how long it took them to do the work and the date it was done.

Double check your invoice

Do not assume that your invoice or fee note is correct. Check it carefully when you receive it and if you've made notes of the work being done, check the invoice against your notes.

Be prepared to challenge anything that does not seem right. Details of how to challenge the invoice should be included in your client care letter.

How to slash your legal bills

A change to the law means that it is possible to cut your legal costs right down by only paying for the services you want, such as individual pieces of work.

This is known as 'unbundling'. Also known as limited-scope representation or pay-as-you-go services, unbundling makes legal fees easier to control – and much more affordable.

With unbundling, you get your lawyer to do some of the legal work for you, but not all of it. And it means you pay for the services of your lawyer when you want them and as you use them. When using unbundling, your lawyer can do as little or as much as you would like them to do.

Here are some reasons why you should consider unbundling:

- Control how much you spend overall
- Agree how much you'll pay, based on each piece of work only
- Avoid a high monthly legal bill
- Avoid having to make a lump sum payment on account (upfront)

- Make the best use of your lawyer's expertise where that expertise is needed most

- Save money by doing any work that you do not require legal knowledge for – such as photocopying, filling in (simple) forms, making telephone calls to the court – yourself

- Have more control over how your case progresses

- Save money by not paying for repetition – for example, after you have given the lawyer information about your case and they write it up, you have to check that it is correct, and pay more for your lawyer to make any corrections.

If you decide to use unbundling, make sure your lawyer agrees to it during that first meeting with you so that they can confirm the arrangement in their follow-up client care letter to you.

SELF CASE STUDY 1

How I filled in a difficult form using unbundling – and saved money

I used unbundling to fill in my form E (the form for a financial order). The form is 28 pages long and the guidance notes are 4 pages long).

Here is my tried and tested method – to use as a guide:

1. Print a blank copy of the form

2. Read through all the questions

3. Mark any questions you do not understand or need help with on your form

4. *Go through the form again (or as many times as you need to) and read the guidance notes to make sure you haven't missed anything*

5. *Book in an hour-long session with your solicitor – tell your solicitor you want to go through sections of your form and that you have specific questions to ask*

6. *Take along the marked-up copy of your form*

7. *Make notes during your session with my solicitor – and write your notes directly onto the form, next to the question the notes relate to*

8. *After the session, type up the answers in the online version of the form*

9. *Save the form as you go along*

10. *Check the form, print off 4 copies and submit it.*

You may wish to fill in a printed copy of the form in pencil and/or if you have more questions for your solicitor, repeat the above steps again.

Going through the form first on my own helped me to understand exactly what the form was about, so that I didn't waste any of the valuable minutes of the hour I had with my solicitor. It also meant that I could start looking for any documents I needed in good time, before submitting the form and before each hearing.

During my session with my solicitor, I took copious notes and wrote all over my form.

Be prepared to dedicate a lot of time to difficult forms (I dedicated more hours than I can remember to my form E, and it was worth it). For example, when filling in form E you will need to collect a lot of documents, including bank statements, mortgage statements, valuations etc. You will need these documents to back-up what you have put in your form.

And it goes without saying that it is best to be truthful on your form.

'Alternative' lawyers

There are other legal services available that can help you cut your legal fees to the minimum.

Here are some options:

Remote or home-based solicitors

Some law firms operate from other locations. Their solicitors do not work in a traditional high street or corporate office, but are instead home-based. Face-to-face meetings are still possible but the majority of the work is done remotely.

This type of arrangement means that without any physical offices to maintain, the overheads are lower and this is reflected in the fees they charge.

If you choose this option, check where the solicitors are based and which court will be dealing with your case. To avoid any misunderstandings or delays, if you have a preference about the location of the court for your hearings, make it clear from the start.

Online advice solicitors

I would describe another model I encountered as online advice solicitors. It involves logging into a website and asking a question. One of that website's solicitors who is available and online at that moment will send you a response.

You get access to a solicitor on a 'piecemeal' basis – and you pay for each question you ask. You may be given the opportunity to ask further questions for a set fee per 'batch' of related questions. I was charged around £20 per question on a legal advice website, but rates do differ.

Worth knowing: If you decide to use this facility, do so with caution. While it may be an option for the odd, simple question, relying solely on this information can be risky.

In my opinion, a piecemeal approach of this nature offers limited value, and in my experience, every answer received was heavily caveated by a statement about the general legal principle which although sound, did not help me in the context of my individual circumstances. Most of each answer I received was taken up with an overall statement about the general legal principle.

If you do use these online advice tools, avoid inputting any personal data into the online systems. Before the General Data Protection Regulation (GDPR) 2018 (legislation to protect how the personal information of individuals is collected and processed), and the updated Data Protection Act (DPA) 2018 came into force, I came across information that others had submitted on one website – and this information was visible to anyone who happened to visit the website, without having to log in securely. With the legal changes of the DPA 2018, this may no longer be an issue, but it is best to be exercise caution.

What to do if you do not have the money right now

If you need advice from a solicitor but do not have the funds immediately available, there is something you can do if you have an asset, such as a property that you own or part-own.

I found myself with this problem and discovered a way around it.

SELF CASE STUDY 2

How I got legal advice without any money

I didn't have any money to meet the full cost of legal fees when I needed legal advice, but I was still able to use the services of a solicitor.

But how?

Here is my tried and tested method – to use as a guide:

I part-owned a property and used that property to come to an agreement with the law firm I used. The agreement was that I would pay my legal fees once I had sold the property.

To do this I had to provide a number of documents to prove:

- *Ownership of the property*

- *How much the property was worth*

- *The outstanding mortgage on the property*

- *That the property was being sold.*

This is an alternative for you if you do not have the money to pay for legal advice when you need it, but you do have money coming to you – whether from the sale of a property or from some other verifiable source.

Discuss your situation with the law firm before your initial face-to-face appointment, to see whether the law firm will agree to such an arrangement in principle. This will give the managing partners at the firm enough time to make a decision – and save you attending the face-to-face appointment if they decide not to accept your proposal.

If they do accept, they will tell you exactly what to bring to your appointment and they will go over the fine details of the payment agreement when you attend their offices.

CHAPTER 5

Representing yourself in court for little or nothing

Every year, since the cuts to legal aid in 2012, more and more people have been going to family court without a lawyer. If you choose to do this, you are known as 'unrepresented' or as a 'litigant in person'.

Judges are becoming more accustomed to dealing with litigants in person and many try as much as possible to accommodate them.

Here are some options to consider, if you're thinking about representing yourself in court.

Doing it yourself

Representing yourself in court and handling all of your own paperwork yourself will save you a lot of money.

It should go without saying that opting for this route will require you to set aside ample time to plan and keep up with everything you need to do.

Carry out as much research as you can, making sure that you verify what you find out from more than one reliable source.

How to manage your paperwork

One of the best pieces of advice I received from a solicitor when I was going to court alone was, "Get a lever arch file and store all of your paperwork in it".

This may seem to be a trivial concern in the greater scheme of things, but as your case progresses, so too will the mountain of paperwork.

Having all of your documents (including copies of original documents and copies of all the documents you have sent to your ex-partner's solicitor and to the court – and bearing in mind that court documents can go missing) labelled and together in one place will make life easier.

Without labelled folders containing your documents, you will struggle to find what you need when you need it, or when you want to add new documents to existing ones in a logical order.

Send your paperwork to the court

In this age of digital communications and electronic storage – it may seem odd that you still have to deal with paperwork, but family courts are still very steeped in tradition and governed by rules.

Changes are afoot, however, and since 7 December 2015, it has been possible to send all enquiries to family courts by email, including family process applications (for example an application for a child arrangements order), plus all letters and all documents that are relevant to a case.

Court bundles (folders of copies of documents that are relevant to a case and prepared for hearings according to Civil Procedure Rules) are excluded.

At the time of writing, court bundles must be printed out, numbered and sent to the court, or hand delivered to the court.

Worth knowing: There is a limit to the physical length and the file size of documents you can send by email to the court. There should be no more than 50 pages in total (including the email itself and all attached documents), and the total file size of the email should be less than 10 MB.

Organise your lever arch file

Here's how to do it:

- Get a lever arch file for each part of your divorce or civil partnership dissolution: one file for the divorce/ dissolution, one for children, and one for finances

- If your case is complicated, you may need more than one lever arch file for sub-topics within each area

- Get subject dividers for each lever arch file

- Add subject names to the dividers in pencil (so that you can easily rub out the section names and change things around as your paperwork inevitably expands). For example, in your finances file you may have a section each for the completed form E, court orders, bank statements, mortgage or rent details, letters, emails, house sale, bills, payslips, P60, credit card statements, savings accounts, evidence of outgoings, pensions valuations etc

- Make sure your documents are in your folders in a consistent order that works best for you. I found that reverse chronological order (with the most recent document at the start of each folder section), worked best for me – because I could easily find what I needed when in court, and I needed to refer to more recent documents the most.

As a litigant in person, you do not have to deal with your paperwork and hearings alone. There are other avenues available to you.

Here are some options to consider:

McKenzie Friends

A McKenzie Friend can help you with your case. McKenzie Friends have existed since the 1970s and operate according to the Civil and Family Courts McKenzie Friend Practice Guidance 2010. They can provide reasonable assistance, moral support, take notes and quietly give you advice during your hearing.

If you have a McKenzie Friend with you when you go to court, you are still classed as a litigant in person by the court. The benefit of having a McKenzie Friend with you is the support you will receive throughout your hearing, at a reduced cost (or, in some cases, for free).

Most paid McKenzie Friends charge low fees for their services, based on an hourly rate or as a set fee for a service, such as attending a hearing.

You should notify the court and the other side about the McKenzie Friend who will be supporting you during your hearing. Before you go into your hearing, your McKenzie Friend will be asked to fill in a McKenzie Friend form and/or to provide a copy of their McKenzie Friend CV.

Your McKenzie can be a friend or distant family member, but if you choose someone you know, they must be objective and must not be directly linked to the case.

Find a McKenzie Friend: http://www.mckenziefriends. directory/index.html

Professional McKenzie Friends

Professional McKenzie Friends will work with you on your case, according to the Civil and Family Courts McKenzie Friend Practice Guidance 2010.

The difference between a Professional McKenzie Friend and a McKenzie Friend is that Professional McKenzie Friends are registered (after meeting qualifying criteria) with the Society of Professional McKenzie Friends and, as a condition of membership, are bound by a code of conduct.

Professional McKenzie Friends must be covered by professional indemnity insurance and must be registered with the Information Commissioner's Office (to ensure they meet their data protection obligations as data controllers), as a condition of their membership of the Society of Professional McKenzie Friends.

If you have a Professional McKenzie Friend with you when you go to court, you will be classed as a litigant in person by the court. Having a Professional McKenzie Friend to support you during your hearing gives you 4 notable benefits: the protection of knowing that he or she is working to a professional code of conduct, is insured, will handle your personal data according to the law and will charge low fees.

You should notify the court and the other side about the Professional McKenzie Friend who will be supporting you during your hearing. Before going into your hearing, your Professional McKenzie Friend will be asked to fill in a McKenzie Friend form and/or provide a copy of their McKenzie Friend CV.

Fees are charged on an hourly basis or as a fixed-fee per service.

Find a Professional McKenzie Friend: https://www.mckenzie-friend.org.uk/mckenzies.html

CLOCK Legal Companions

CLOCK (Community Legal Outreach Keele) Legal Companions are trained student volunteers who are studying for their law degree. They offer free legal help and support to litigants in person.

CLOCK Legal Companions may be available at a court near you. They can help you with your court paperwork, attend hearings with you and give you information about specialist organisations that may be able to give you further assistance.

Ask about the service at your local court, and go to the CLOCK desk or room to get free help.

Personal Support Unit Volunteers

The Personal Support Unit (PSU) works with charities and provides trained volunteers to help litigants in person – based in courts in England and Wales.

PSU volunteers provide support and practical help including explaining how courts work, helping with form filling, organising paperwork and working with you to plan what to say in court. PSU Volunteers can also help you find out whether you can get free legal advice.

Find your local PSU: https://www.thepsu.org

CHAPTER 6
Where to get free legal advice

There are many organizations that offer free legal advice in England and Wales.

Here is a selection:

Law Centres Network – England

The Law Centres Network service can put you in touch with individually-run, community-based law centres. Some of the centres offer free legal advice on family matters.

Use the law centres network list to find a centre near you: http://www.lawcentres.org.uk/

South West London Law Centre

The South West London Law Centre is part of the Law Centre Network and offers free legal advice on family law to those who live, work or study in parts of the south London area. The centre offers daytime and evening advice sessions.

To find your centre in south London and the centre opening hours, visit: http://www.swllc.org/

Child Law Advice

Child Law Advice is a registered charity that offers legal advice and information on family and child law. The charity provides telephone-based intensive support for complex cases. Calls are charged at local rate.

To find out about Child Law Advice's legal advice services, visit: http://childlawadvice.org.uk

Citizen's Advice

There is a Citizen's Advice Bureau (CAB) in most towns in England and Wales. Your local CAB offers free drop-in sessions and telephone-based advice. CAB will organise follow-up sessions for in-depth advice and can signpost you to other services and organisations.

CAB also has a wealth of online advice.

Contact the national CAB telephone advice line or chat online to an advisor: http://www.citizensadvice.org.uk

Pro bono assistance

The Latin phrase 'pro bono (publico)' means 'for the public good' and is used as shorthand for free legal advice.

Barristers and solicitors who work pro bono do so without receiving payment for their professional advice.

The following organisations offer pro bono advice:

LawWorks
A charity that provides access to solicitors who offer pro bono legal advice to individuals.

http://lawworks.org.uk/clinics

Advocate
Advocate provides free legal help by matching barristers who undertake pro bono work with individuals who need help but cannot pay for it.

Individuals have to be referred to the service by an advice agency (for example a law centre, legal advice centre or Citizens Advice Bureau – see above) and it is up to the agency to decide whether or not to refer a case to Advocate.

https://weareadvocate.org.uk/

Birmingham University: Free Legal Advice Group
The Free Legal Advice Group (FLAG), is run by students of the university, who, after attending training, give advice under the supervision of qualified legal professionals.

FLAG also runs advice clinics.

http://www.birmingham.ac.uk/schools/law/flag/about.aspx

Law Clinic at Swansea University
Trained law students provide free initial legal advice to members of the public, by appointment only. Students work alongside practising lawyers.

https://www.swansea.ac.uk/law/lawclinic/#accept

University of Law
Available throughout England and in Wales.

Pro bono legal advice is provided to members of the public by postgraduate students of the university who are training to become solicitors or barristers. Their work is supervised by experienced lawyers.

http://www.law.ac.uk/about/legal-advice-for-the-public

University of Reading: School of Law
Students of the university work as advisors in legal advice centres under the supervision of qualified solicitors during advice sessions.

http://www.reading.ac.uk/law/undergraduate-degrees/pro-bono.aspx

Other sources of free legal advice

There are many other options available to you if you're looking for free legal advice.

Here are some to begin with:

Free law firm advice

While it is true that law firms charge a fee for advice, some do offer some advice for free, but may not necessarily publicise that fact.

——

SELF CASE STUDY 3

How I got free legal advice from 4 solicitors

At the start of my journey, I had no idea what to do first or in what order to do things, and I had very little money to spare. I had no idea which law firm to use.

Here is my tried and tested method – for you to use as a guide:

- *Summarise the issue you need help with (doing this on paper works for most people)*

- *Draw up a shortlist of questions, around 3 or 4 should do. List your questions in order of priority (in case you do not get to ask them all)*

- *Do some online research and pick around 6 local law firms that offer a free initial telephone consultation (some firms offer this but do not publicise it, so do make contact with law firms that haven't explicitly ruled it out)*

- *Call each of the law firms on your list and follow the next steps for each one*

- *Pick a solicitor to talk to; preferably someone senior – most firms will have solicitors' profiles listed on their websites.*

- *Explain the circumstances of your case succinctly*

- *Say that you have a couple of questions to ask and then ask away*

- *Ask the solicitor what they think you should do*

- *Ask them how they work and what you would need to do to have them represent you.*

When I tried this, all 4 solicitors I spoke to advised me to do exactly the same thing. Not only did this provide me with the reassurance I needed and confirmation of what to do next, but it didn't cost me a penny.

Worth knowing: This option is good for initial advice, or for an answer to a fairly straightforward question. When using this option, weigh up the information you receive in the context of your personal situation and the details of your case.

Legal resources

Advice Now
This website has an extensive range of online information with free basic guides. There is also a wide selection of in-depth premium guides for sale.

https://www.advicenow.org.uk

Moneyworks Brighton & Hove
This advice agency runs an advice line and provides drop-in appointments for local residents across the city for help with money management.

https://www.advicebrighton-hove.org.uk/#contact

National Debt Line
Free debt advice and information are available from National Debt Line. The charity also has online tools, including a budget calculator that can be filled in online, saved and downloaded.

https://www.nationaldebtline.org

Shelter

Shelter is a housing and homelessness charity. Contact Shelter's advice line or use their online chat for help from expert housing advisers. You will find general housing advice on Shelter's website.

https://england.shelter.org.uk/get_help

AFTERWORD

You've reached the end of this book and may already have had the opportunity to use, or plan how to use some of the many ideas presented here, to help you save thousands during your divorce or dissolution.

I originally wrote this book four years ago, partly as a collection of thoughts and 'how tos', partly as friendly advice about everything relating to the divorce process, as I experienced it. When I looked back over my drafts last year, I realised that there was a pervading theme throughout: money. This theme tallies with what the overwhelming majority of my clients who contact me for McKenzie Friend services tell me.

Saving money during this phase of life tends not to be something that is widely discussed; and it should be.

Getting the divorce or the dissolution, plus the effect of all the incidents that led to the end of the relationship often leave little room for anything else.

The divorce or dissolution becomes 'the end' (and the goal is to reach the end at any cost). But why not flip that approach on its head?

Thinking back to my own journey, I remember a point when I started to see the end goal as laying the foundations for a new life and from that point on, I was more motivated than ever to find ways to save money.

Your own journey may follow a similar path to my own, or a very different one. But whichever path your journey takes, what better way to start that new chapter of your life, with more money, rather than less?

I hope, in some small way this book will have contributed towards enriching that new chapter of your life.

Debbie Thomas, 25th March 2019

LIST OF RESOURCES MENTIONED

Save time and money by quickly finding the resources mentioned throughout this book.

You can download the full list of resources online from: http://www.goingtocourtalone.co.uk/resources/

Resources

Fill in a CAFCASS parenting plan
https://www.cafcass.gov.uk/grown-ups/parents-and-carers/divorce-and-separation/parenting-plan

Check whether you can get legal aid
https://www.gov.uk/check-legal-aid

Find a legal aid adviser or mediator
https://find-legal-advice.justice.gov.uk

See the full list of court fees
https://www.gov.uk/government/publications/fees-in-the-civil-and-family-courts-main-fees-ex50

Apply for help with court fees
https://www.gov.uk/government/publications/apply-for-help-with-court-and-tribunal-fees#details

See a full list of court forms
https://www.gov.uk/government/collections/court-and-tribunal-forms

Apply for a council tax reduction
https://www.gov.uk/apply-council-tax-reduction

Child maintenance

Estimate your child maintenance contributions
https://www.gov.uk/calculate-your-child-maintenance

Use Child Maintenance Options for your child maintenance agreement
https://www.cmoptions.org/en/maintenance/

Pensions

Find lost pensions (Pension Tracing Service)
https://www.gov.uk/find-pension-contact-details

Find out how much is in your pension (get a pension valuation)
https://www.pensionwise.gov.uk/en/pension-pot-value

Options for dividing up your pension
https://www.moneyadviceservice.org.uk/en/articles/dividing-pensions-on-divorce-or-dissolution

Apply for a valuation of a state pension
https://www.gov.uk/government/publications/application-for-a-state-pension-forecast-on-divorce-or-dissolution-br20

Speak to a financial adviser (about your pension options)
https://register.fca.org.uk/

Arbitration

Family arbitrators
http://ifla.org.uk

Mediation

Family mediators
https://www.familymediationcouncil.org.uk/find-local-mediator/

Emotional support

Dealing with:

Relationship and family problems
https://www.samaritans.org/how-we-can-help-you/
contact-us/what-speak-us-about

Domestic and psychological abuse – women (and children)
https://www.womensaid.org.uk/

Domestic violence advice and support – men
http://www.mensadviceline.org.uk/

Domestic abuse support – LGBT
https://lgbt.foundation/how-we-can-help-you/domestic-abuse

Legal advice from lawyers

Collaborative lawyers
http://www.resolution.org.uk/findamember/

Direct-access barristers
www.barcouncil.org.uk/publicaccess

Solicitors
http://solicitors.lawsociety.org.uk

Chartered Legal Executives
https://www.cilex.org.uk/about_cilex/about-cilex-lawyers/
cilex-practitioners-directory

Legal assistance/advice

McKenzie Friends
http://www.mckenziefriends.directory/index.html

Professional McKenzie Friends
https://www.mckenzie-friend.org.uk/mckenzies.html

Personal Support Unit Volunteers
https://www.thepsu.org

Law Centres Network – England
http://www.lawcentres.org.uk/

South West London Law Centre
http://www.swllc.org/

Child Law Advice
http://childlawadvice.org.uk

Citizen's Advice
http://www.citizensadvice.org.uk

Pro bono advice

Advocate
https://weareadvocate.org.uk

LawWorks
http://lawworks.org.uk/clinics

Birmingham University: Free Legal Advice Group
http://www.birmingham.ac.uk/schools/law/flag/about.aspx

Law Clinic at Swansea University
https://www.swansea.ac.uk/law/lawclinic/#accept

University of Law (throughout England & Wales)
http://www.law.ac.uk/about/legal-advice-for-the-public/

University of Reading: School of Law
http://www.reading.ac.uk/law/undergraduate-degrees/
pro-bono.aspx

Legal/extra resources

Advice Now
https://www.advicenow.org.uk

Moneyworks Brighton & Hove
https://www.advicebrighton-hove.org.uk/#contact

National Debt Line
https://www.nationaldebtline.org/

Shelter
https://england.shelter.org.uk/get_help

ACKNOWLEDGEMENTS

Stop Paying Out! would not have been possible without the help and support of everyone who has been by my side on this amazing journey into print.

In particular, I would like to thank my wonderful test readers: Mum, Tats and Arianne.

Thank you to my editor, Marlon Cameron, whose eye for detail and editorial finessing have been invaluable.

Special thanks go to Charlotte Delmonte for the cover design and page layout – and for steering me along the right creative path. https://charlottedelmonte.co.uk

And lastly, a very big thank you to all whose unflinching support has remained steadfast over the years.

Thank you!

GLOSSARY

Arbitration

A form of dispute resolution. Sessions are run by family justice professionals (arbitrators) with the aim of settling a dispute between two parties.

Bundle

A folder containing documents that are relevant to a case. A bundle is prepared in readiness for a hearing.

CAFCASS
(Children and Family Court Advisory and Support Service)

The body that represents children in family court cases in England. It has a duty to safeguard and promote the welfare of children in the family justice system.

CAFCASS CYMRU
(Children and Family Court Advisory and Support Service Wales)

The body that represents children in family court cases in Wales. It has a duty to safeguard and promote the welfare of children in the family justice system.

CGT
(Capital Gains Tax)

A tax that is payable when you sell an asset (e.g. a second property that is not your main residence) that has increased in value since you bought it. The amount of CGT payable is based on the size of the gain and your income.

CAO
(Child arrangements order)

A court order which stipulates who a child will live with, spend time with or have contact with. This order replaces the 'residence order' and contact order'.

CETV
(Cash equivalent transfer value)

The lump-sum equivalent of your pension. The sum of money your pension scheme administrators will offer in exchange for you giving up a future claim for pension rights from the scheme.

Civil and Family Courts McKenzie Friend Practice Guidance 2010

Guidance for family and civil cases which sets out the rights of litigants in person (those going to court without legal representation), and what a McKenzie Friend is allowed and not allowed to do.

Clean break order

This order legally ends all financial ties between you and your ex-partner and prevents any future financial claims being made by either of you.

Conditional order

A provisional order of the court that confirms you are entitled (as the applicant) to bring a civil partnership to an end.

Consent order

This is an order issued by a judge where you and your ex-partner have both agreed on a financial settlement and consent to an order about how you will divide up assets (e.g. property and savings) between you, without the need for a court hearing.

Council tax reduction

This is a reduction (of up to 100%) in your council tax that you may be entitled to, if you are on a low income or receive benefits. Formerly known as council tax benefit.

Data controller

A person who decides what personal data (of another person) is processed or is to be processed and how to handle or process the personal data.

DPA 2018
(Data Protection Act 2018)

This Act controls how personal information is used in the UK by government, organisations and businesses. It implements the GDPR 2018 (General Data Protection Regulation 2018) and ensures that information is used fairly, lawfully and in a transparent way.

Decree absolute

The legal document that confirms a marriage has legally ended.

Decree nisi

A provisional order of the court that confirms you are entitled (as the applicant) to bring a marriage to an end. You are still legally married at this stage.

Dispute resolution

Refers to a process of resolving a dispute or disagreement between parties and can include negotiation, mediation, arbitration or collaborative law.

Dissipating assets

Disposing of assets – usually with the aim of trying to hide assets in financial proceedings.

Dissolution
(Civil partnership dissolution)

The ending of a civil partnership.

FCA
(Financial Conduct Authority)

Regulates the financial conduct of financial services firms and markets.

Final order

The legal document that confirms that a civil partnership has legally ended.

Financial association

This is a financial link that is created between you and another person when you apply for a joint financial product such as a mortgage or bank account.

Financial disassociation

This removes any financial link or association between you and another person (such as an ex-partner).

Financial disclosure

Where both of you provide full details of your financial positions to each other. Also known as full and frank disclosure.

Financial order

A court order that stipulates how your money and assets will be divided (formerly known as ancillary relief).

Forensic accountant

A specialist accountant who investigates financial irregularities and advises on the financial aspects of disputes.

Freezing order

An order in financial proceedings to prevent assets being disposed of.

GDPR 2018
(General Data Protection Regulation 2018)

A regulation in EU law on data protection and privacy for all individuals in the European Union and the European Economic Area.

ICO
(Information Commissioner's Office)

Regulatory body responsible for monitoring and regulating data protection issues and obligations.

Judicial separation

This is a legal separation for those whose marriage has lasted for less than a year.

Legal aid

Help from the government to meet the cost of legal advice, family mediation and representation in court.

Limited-scope representation

An arrangement whereby a lawyer works on some parts of a case only, for a set fee or limited fees.

Maintenance order

This is an order for ongoing payments by one spouse to the other after the end of the marriage or civil partnership. Also known as spousal maintenance.

Mediator (family)

A family mediator is an independent and professionally trained mediator who can work with you and your ex-partner to help you reach an agreement about issues you are dealing with.

MIAM
(Mediation Information Assessment Meeting)

This is the first mediation appointment that must take place before you take your case to court. It is run by a certified mediator (who holds a Family Mediation Council Accreditation).

Non-molestation order

A court order that prevents one person from using or making a threat of violence against another person – or intimidating, harassing or contacting them.

Occupation order

An interim (short-term) court order that states who can go to or occupy the family home (or occupy specific parts of the family home).

Parenting plan

This an agreement between you and your child's other

parent about arrangements for your children, including who your child will live with, and contact arrangements with the non-resident parent.

PRR
(Private residence relief)

A special relief on second properties that allows interim owners of second properties to sell the property within a certain timeframe to avoid having to pay an additional tax (Capital Gains Tax).

Separation order

This is a legal separation for those ending a marriage or civil partnership that has lasted for less than a year.

Single person council tax discount

The discount you are entitled to receive on your council tax bill if you are the only adult living in a household (the reduction is set at 25%).

Spousal maintenance

This is an order for ongoing payments by one spouse to the other after the end of the marriage or civil partnership. Also known as maintenance.

Unbundling

An arrangement whereby a lawyer works on some parts of a case only, for a set fee or limited fees, by agreement.

INDEX

38739076R00049

Printed in Poland
by Amazon Fulfillment
Poland Sp. z o.o., Wrocław